The CREATIVE ADVENTURES Book 2

Written by Rosana Azar

Edited by Bess Gutter

Silver Spring, MD

WWW.ARTINYOU.COM

Published by Creative Adventures.
Silver Spring, MD

ISBN: 978-1-387-19912-9

CREATIVE ADVENTURES 2017

For use by families, teachers, homeschool
teachers, and after school teachers, and for
anyone else who would love to be inspired.

Dedication

To my daughter Talia, and my
son Damian, for always being
my number one fans.

TABLE OF CONTENTS

ABOUT THIS BOOK

The purpose of this book is to share and to inspire creativity.

It's beyond the results itself, it's the process, the doing, the creative mind activated.

Each person is unique in his or her own imagination. Everybody has to find his or her own expressive way.

There is no wrong or right way.

The most important part of the art creation is the trying, being curious, thinking outside the box, and being surprised by the process.

Let's leave the art critic out of it, and allow ourselves to enjoy and play with these wonderful lessons.

Let's have fun and share it too.

And don't forget to check us out at www.artinyou.org to see learn more about our art programs, community involvement, and of course ideas and inspiration.

Thank you for believing in yourself, and your students.

Have fun!

Rosana Azar
Author and Creator

BEST PRACTICES

The following are tips and teacher hacks to use in your space to keep everything organized and tidy.

Use cheap plastic table coverings to put over tables before materials and students make an appearance. This will make clean up easier. You can likely find these at your local grocery store.

Take a household sponge and cut it into small 2" squares. When using paint and brushes, give each student a sponge. Instruct students to wash their brush off when they're done with one color, dry their brush on the sponge (so that their paint won't be watery), and then choose a new color.

Often, you might find that the paint has not had enough time to dry on some projects. Encourage students to always start with the lightest colors (that way they can always use darker colors).

When using white glue (such as Elmer's), put a little bit of glue into a bottle cap, and have student use a paintbrush to apply. This keeps students from using too much, which can often be messy and takes longer to dry.

Use a crab claw cracker to open tough glue caps. You can also pre-soak the glue caps in vegetable oil to keep them from sticking.

Use condiment bottles for easy paint dispensing.

Help paintbrushes last longer by washing them with hair conditioner.

For a reusable paint palette, glue bottle caps upside-down on a plastic lid from a coffee tin.

For a disposable palette, use take-out condiment containers that you'd find at your local grocery store. Use the lids to keep your supplies from spilling when transporting.

When you have a collection of broken crayons that are too small to use, separate them by color in a muffin tin (if they still have their paper on them, soak the crayons in warm water until the paper starts to come off with ease). Put the muffin tray in the oven at 275 degrees for 7-8 minutes to melt down the bits into new crayons. Keep a close eye on them while they're in the oven, as they melt quickly.

To rescue a dried up Sharpie, place the tip in rubbing alcohol until a bit of ink starts to come out. Replace the cap and let the pen sit for at least 15 minutes.

If you're using messy materials with lots of little pieces, give students the tops to cardboard boxes that reams of paper would be delivered in, or disposable baking tins. They can do their work inside their trays, keeping any excess mess in one place.

To clean dirty chalk pastels, place them in a bag of rice and shake them around.

To clean dirty or hard erasers, rub the area against an emery board.

Make sure to give students plenty of warnings before class ends to help them keep track of the remaining time.

Establish a relationship with a nearby picture framer, and ask them if they'd be willing to donate mat board scraps

Visit the "Materials" section of our website for more ideas: www.artinyou.org

THINK OUTSIDE THE BOX

Aboriginal Masks

MATERIALS:

Cardboard circles

Pencils

Black permanent markers

Samples of Zentangles

Extra cardboard pieces

Colored tissue paper

Glue

Brushes

Glue gun and glue sticks

SUMMARY Students will decorate circular masks using a variety of materials and patterns.

PURPOSE To learn more about Aboriginal art work and culture.

VOCAB Aboriginal, Zentangle, repeat, pattern, bridge (as it pertains to the nose)

BEHIND THE MASK

Throughout history, Aboriginal masks have been used for a variety of reasons, including ceremonies, rituals, dances, and to honor the spirits. Located in the most northern part of Australia, Cape York is home to a tribe that uses masks for important ceremonial dances.

CARDBOARD CIRCLES

Although it's possible to cut the cardboard circles needed for this activity, it's easier to buy cardboard cake rounds from any local craft store. They should be between 12" and 14" inches in diameter.

1. See photos on the previous page for an idea of how the eyes and nose bridge will be cut out. This should be done ahead of time. The bottom cut will sit on the bridge of the student's nose like a pair of glasses. NOTE: Keep all scrap cardboard; students will use that later to decorate their masks.

2. Once each student has their own mask, they will draw repeating lines and patterns with a black permanent marker to make their mask unique.

3. Using any tissue paper or leftover cardboard scraps, students can continue to add to their masks for three-dimensional effects.

THINK OUTSIDE THE BOX

Alien Names

MATERIALS:

- Bristol/Card stock or cardboard paper (white)
- Pencils
- Erasers
- Oil pastels
- Glue
- Black construction paper

SUMMARY Students will use their names to create unique alien-like creatures.

PURPOSE To have a greater appreciation and pride for ones name.

VOCAB alien, oil pastels, contour, crease

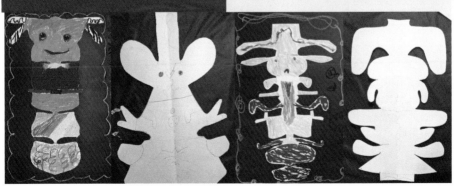

DIFFERENT PAPERS

There are many types of paper you can choose from for this lesson. One option is Bristol paper, which is also known as card stock. You may also use cardboard paper but it has less sheen to it. Both types of paper are thicker than regular printer paper, so make sure students crease their paper enough that it lies flat.

1. Give each student a piece of thick paper (card stock or cardboard paper), and have them fold the paper in half, the long way (hot dog style).

2. Have students write their name in large letters, with the folded side closest to their body. Make sure the bottom of the letters touches the folded crease.

3. Instruct students to draw a contour line around the top of the letters (it helps if you keep your pencil on the paper the whole time, never lifting it up). Next, students will cut along that line.

4. When they open up their name, they will find a unique shape that, with a little imagination, can resemble the body of a monster or alien.

5. Students will add features and details (e.g., face, clothing, shoes, etc.) and complete their figure with oil pastels.

6. To make an exciting presentation, they can mount their alien/monsters on the black construction paper when it's done.

7. If there is time, students can make additional figures using names of family or friends.

THINK OUTSIDE THE BOX

Fazzino Boxes

MATERIALS:

Sample paint strips from hardware store in a variety of colors

4x4 Boxes you can buy online, like gift boxes, or cardboard boxes

Black permanent markers

Foam pieces for spacers

Glue

Glue brushes

Markers

SUMMARY Students will create a collage/mosaic on four sides of a box using a variety of materials and imagery.

PURPOSE To learn more about Charles Fazzino, one of the most well-known 3-D Pop Artists.

VOCAB three-dimensional, pop art

ABOUT CHARLES FAZZINO

Charles Fazzino graduated from the School of Visual Arts in NYC, and has been a pop-artist for over 30 years. Much of his artwork is a reflection of his childhood in NYC, and the many sights throughout the city. As a child, he enjoyed riding public transportation, and this served as inspiration for his art. The images he comes up with are like books; they tell a story. Fazzino uses a variety of materials, such as glitter and rhinestones, to really make his artwork pop.

USING OUR MEMORY

When having students come up with the imagery to be used for this project, ask them to brainstorm a written list of places they have been. For example: a specific part of his or her neighborhood, a place they visit during their favorite season, maybe a room in a house or building, or a famous buildings like the White House, or the Empire State Building.

1. Students will come up with 4 scenes that they can create by visualizing.

2. They will recreate each scene on each face of the box using the collage materials. If boxes are not available, you can also make a three-sided triangle, with the base mounted on cardboard, mat board, or card stock (students will then use three scenes, not four).

3. Show students how to create space by making each layer rise above the paper with the foam shapes to add a shadow effect, and making their artwork three-dimensional.

4. Students may decorate the boxes to add features and details, and to express their ideas and feelings about the place. They can use as much or as little material as needed.

5. As students start to finish, have them pair with a classmate to talk about their different scenery, and why they chose the imagery they did.

THINK OUTSIDE THE BOX

Romero Britto

MATERIALS:

1 Canvas per student

Scrap paper

Tempera paint

Paint brushes

Black pencils

Black permanent markers

Water containers

Small sponge squares

SUMMARY Using paints and other materials, students will create artwork inspired by artist Romero Britto.

PURPOSE To learn more about the art of Romero Britto, while working on their spatial skills.

VOCAB segment, divide, overlap

ABOUT ROMERO BRITTO

Romero Britto was born in Brazil but spent much of his life in Miami. His style of artwork includes bright colors, thick outlines of shapes and symbols, and a general vibe of happiness and vibrancy that he feels towards life. Britto taught himself to create artwork at a young age using paper scraps and eventually traveled to Paris to continue his art education. His biggest influences are Matisse and Picasso. If you look Britto up online, you can see many examples of his artwork that inspire this lesson.

IMAGINING SYMBOLS

If a student is having difficulty designing symbols, have them come up with a place and describe all the things that they see there, and you or the student can write down a list as they come up with ideas.

1. Students will begin their design by drawing a large character or symbol. Next, have them divide the space into numerous segments. Encourage them to experiment with this on scrap paper first.

2. When they are satisfied with their layout for the base design, they will draw it larger on the canvas provided

3. Next, students will outline their images with black permanent marker while making sure there are lines of different thickness

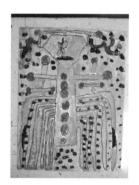

4. After outlining, they can begin painting. Suggest that they begin with the lightest colors first, as this is easier than beginning with the darkest colors.

5. Once every segment is painted with a solid base color, they can go back with another color and create different designs on top of it.

THINK OUTSIDE THE BOX

Built Up Relief

MATERIALS:

Scissors
Pencils
Glue
Glue brushes
Mat board bases
Manila folder pieces
Paper towels or sponge pieces
Green scrubbing sponge
Glue containers
Shoe polish
Aluminum foil

SUMMARY   Students will create metallic artwork inspired by Cesar Domela.

PURPOSE   To learn more about the artwork and methods that Cesar Domela used.

VOCAB   Overlap, layers, crease, relief

ABOUT CESAR DOMELA

Cesar was born in Amsterdam, Netherlands. He started painting at the age of 18 and devoted the rest of his life to art. In 1923, he showed his first abstract artwork in Berlin at the exhibition named the 'November Group.' Later in life, he started to experiment with different materials such as wood, brass, copper, glass, etc.

FRIEND A FRAMER

Looking for cheap or free mat board? Become good friends with a local picture framer. Often times they will discard mat board scraps. Ask if they'll donate these materials to your classroom instead.

1. Students will begin by stacking the manilla folders in layers to create a raised effect, making a pronounced relief (no more than 6 layers, and no less than 2). Have the students use glue to overlap shapes, starting with the largest on the bottom to the smallest on the top. This will achieve a layered effect.

2. Once complete, demonstrate how to cover their artwork with aluminum foil by gently but firmly pressing so they can see all the different layers.

3. Next, students will add shoe polish using either a paper towel or sponge pieces.

4. Once the shoe polish has been applied, students will use the green scrubbing sponge to create texture and enhance the creases and create contrast between the shiny and black areas.

THINK OUTSIDE THE BOX

Fabric Construction

MATERIALS:

Mat board bases
Mat board shapes
Glue gun and sticks
Fabric
Scissors
Glue
Masking tape
Wire
Beads
Yarn
Sequins
Ribbons
Any other scraps of material

SUMMARY Students will learn to use a variety of materials, including cloth, to create a textile composition.

PURPOSE To gain an understanding of how art can be made with any material.

VOCAB textile, composition

NO BRAINSTORMING

Although most lessons require considerable planning before using materials, this lesson is not one of them! The focus of this project is to challenge students to discover where their creativity can lead them. The artwork that results does not have to depict a recognizable subject, but might be a vibrant collection of colorful materials.

1. Each student will begin with a mat board base of any size, which they will wrap in fabric.

2. Students will take a few more smaller mat board shapes and wrap those in different fabric and textiles. They can use the wire, sequins, yarn, ribbons, beads, or any other material available to create layers and texture.

3. Students will use these shapes and their larger mat board piece to create 3-D textile artwork. It can be a whimsical landscape, or a collection of shapes and colors. Students can create any arrangement, whether abstract or recognizable.

HANDS ON ART
Mandalas

MATERIALS:

White card stock/bristol paper

Colored pencils

Black paper

Scissors

Glue

Regular sized plate (can be paper)

SUMMARY Students will learn what a mandala is, and draw one using their own hands as stencils.

PURPOSE To gain an appreciation for both the culture of mandalas, as well as the unique shape of their own hands.

VOCAB mandala, henna, intersect

WHAT IS A MANDALA?

The word 'mandala' is Sanskrit for 'circle' and has origins in the Hindu, Buddhism, and Jainism religions. Mandala's represent devotion to their religious culture. They can be represented using a variety of different materials, such as paint, wood, canvas, fabric, etc. Featuring a variety of shapes, patterns, and symbols, mandalas are used for having spiritual interactions with the many different religious deities.

AHEAD OF TIME

Make sure to draw the circles on white paper <u>before</u> teaching this lesson. Use a paper plate or real plate as a stencil. To help students create some unique artwork, you can print out some examples of different henna designs for inspiration.

1. Using colored pencils, the children will start tracing their hands inside of the circle, overlapping it and creating interesting designs.

2. Next, they will start coloring each piece with different colors. With the overlapping, this will create different segments to be colored. Encourage students to blend and layer colors where they intersect.

3. If there's time, students can create a border or frame using the black paper. For this, students will cut out their mandala, and will glue it to black paper.

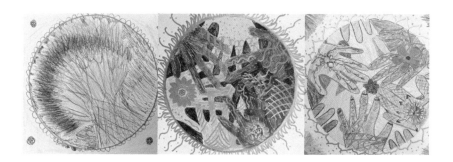

HANDS ON ART
Deconstructed Hand

MATERIALS:

Brightly colored construction paper

Scissors

Pencils

Glue

Glue brushes

SUMMARY Students will create a unique shape using a traced cutout of their hand and arm.

PURPOSE To see how one shape can become something completely different.

VOCAB complimentary, reconstruct, horizontal

COMPLIMENTARY COLORS

Try to choose the construction paper based on complimentary colors. For example, yellow and orange may be too similar in color for either of them to stand out, but yellow and purple are contrasting enough to create a vibrant piece of unique artwork. Other examples of complimentary colors could include red/ green, blue/ orange, yellow/ pink, purple/ orange, and so on.

1. Each student will be given two pieces of brightly colored construction paper. The two colors should contrast enough to be complimentary to each other.

2. On one piece of paper, the student will trace his or her hand, all the way up their elbow. Next, they will cut this shape out. The other colored construction paper will be their base.

3. Have students add lines to the hand and arm (but not fingers) and in- between the lines, students should carefully number the segments, going in order from either top to bottom, or bottom to top. This will help them reconstruct the shapes in the order they appeared originally. When this is completed, the students will cut along these lines to divide the original shape into segments.

4. Next, students will reconstruct their shape, leaving space in between each cut-out. They should make sure the numbered side is facing down so as not to be seen.

5. Using the extra scrap paper from their cut- out shape, students can create a unique piece of art that can feature an animal, alien, a favorite scene, etc.

HANDS ON ART
Surrealistic Hands

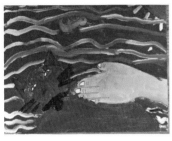

MATERIALS:

Black pencils
Tempera
Canvas
Brushes
Water containers
Paint containers
Sponges

SUMMARY — Students create sculptures inspired by Salvador Dali's surrealism.

PURPOSE — To gain an appreciation for Dali's most signature form of artwork: surrealism.

VOCAB — surrealism, composition

ABOUT SALVADOR DALI

Dali was born on May 11, 1904, in Figueres, Spain. He was very interested in art as a child. His parents eventually enrolled him at the Academia de San Fernando in Madrid in 1922, however, he was permanently expelled right before taking his final exams because he declared that no teacher was a good enough artist to rightfully judge his work. Eventually, he joined the surrealist movement, using a mental exercise that he called the "paranoiac-critical method" where he would use his dreams and subconscious thought to create an alternate reality. His art has even found its way into films, such as Alfred Hitchcock's Spellbound (1945). Dali stopped painting at the age of 80 when he was forced to retire because of a motor disorder that rendered his hands useless.

1. For this lesson, students will work on the canvas they have been provided. Using a black pencil, they will trace their hands onto the canvas. They can position their hands anywhere: centered, to one side, upside down, etc.

2. Using their hands as starting points, students are encouraged to use their imaginations to create a scene or composition in a surrealistic manner. The images can be attached or unattached to their hands. The image can make sense or not.

3. Once the students have their scenes drawn out with pencil, they can add paint to their artwork. Encourage students to use bold colors, as Dali often did.

HANDS ON ART
Finger Printing

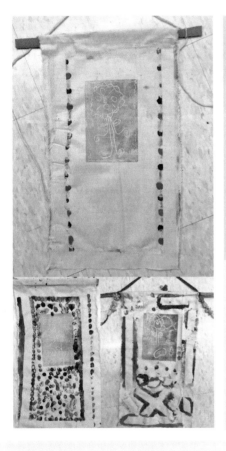

MATERIALS:
Muslin
Styrofoam plate
Printing ink
Brayers rollers
Tempera
Black permanent markers
Dowels
Glue gun
Masking tape
Yarn
Ribbon
Beads

SUMMARY
Students will create fingerprint and foam printed artwork on fabric.

PURPOSE
To learn more about using different materials to create patterned artwork.

VOCAB
muslin, transfer, impression

ABOUT ED EMBERLY

Ed Emberley was born on October 19, 1931 in Malden, Massachusetts. He attended the Massachusetts College of Art and Design where he received a Bachelor in Fine Arts degree in painting and illustration. He also spent some time at the well-known Rhode Island School of Design. Emberly is most famous for his instructional drawing books geared towards children. He believed that anyone can learn to draw. His step-by-step instructions make it easy for children to follow along. He even uses fingerprints to create drawings of animals, people, etc.

MIRRORED IMAGES

When students are initially drawing their scenes, they need to keep in mind that the printed image will be reversed. For example, if they're using numbers or letters, these need to be written backwards. To see more videos on how this is done, head over to our YouTube page to see featured content that demonstrates the methods used in this lesson.

1. Each student will be given a styrofoam 'printing' plate, where they will eventually design a scene, symbol, treasure, etc. First, have students come up with their drawing on scrap paper. Once they have their image drawn out, they will transfer it to the foam plate by taping the paper over the foam and gently drawing over the original image. Make sure to press firmly but not enough to rip the paper or foam. This will leave an engraved image that will be used as a stamp. Students may need to go over the engraved areas to deepen the impression.

2. Using the brayer and tempera paints, students will paint over the engraved side. Making sure the painted foam design is facing up, students will carefully place the fabric on top, using pressure to transfer the ink to the fabric. Try to keep the image away from the edges, and more towards the middle sections.

3. Once this part has been completed, students can use masking tape to create borders by painting over the tape, and using ink pads and their fingerprints to make patterned designs around their printed image.

4. The teacher will create a hanger by gluing the top fold over a wooden dowel and tying a long piece of yarn to each end. Students can continue to decorate their fabric with ribbon and beads.

HANDS ON ART
Hold the World

MATERIALS:

Mat boards	Brushes for glue
Paper cups	Glue gun
Die-cut hands	Glue sticks
Foam shapes	Scissors
Woodsies	Pencils
Pipe cleaners	Erasers
Colored paper	Permanent markers
Glue	

SUMMARY Students will represent what the world would look like if it were in their hands.

PURPOSE To expand the imagination by picturing a unique world that is entirely the creation of the student.

VOCAB diorama, represent, three-dimensional

WHAT'S IN YOUR WORLD?

Allow students to really use the materials how they see fit. They can cut their paper cup in a spiral, or maybe like petals. Their cut-out hands can be either on the cup or on the mat board. They can imagine a candy world, or a toy world, or a world with beautiful trees and flowers. What kind of animals live in this world, if any? Are there any buildings, bodies of water, deserts, jungles, etc?

1. Each student will be given a mat board and up to 3 paper cups that they will cut and open up. If you are able to provide cups of various sizes and colors, this will help students with their creative expressions. Using the scissors, they will cut up the paper cups into different shapes, and glue their piece or pieces to the mat board, giving their artwork a three dimensional aspect. The glue gun should be used for this part, and operated by an adult.

2. Give each student one or two hands, and have them glue the hands either on the cup, or on the mat board. You can either use a die-cut or trace a set of small hands (maybe a student's) and cut them out ahead of time.

3. Using the various materials (foam shapes, woodsies, pipe cleaners, colored paper), students will decorate their artwork, representing a world that they imagined. They can draw more designs with a pencil, and go over them with permanent markers.

HANDS ON ART
Glove Puppets

MATERIALS:
Fabric gloves
Newspaper
Fabric
Googly eyes
Pom-poms
Beads
Scissors
Disposable plastic grocery bags
Ribbons
Yarn
Permanent markers
Glue gun
Glue sticks
Wire

SUMMARY Students will create a puppet out of gardening gloves and various other materials.

PURPOSE To learn how to use various materials to make a puppet.

VOCAB puppet

30

GARDENING GLOVES

You can purchase fabric gloves at cheap prices from any hardware or gardening store. They are usually made of a canvas material, which makes them easier to decorate. To understand how the puppets are made, head to our YouTube page and check out our videos for this lesson.

1. Each student will be given one fabric glove. First, instruct the students to tuck the thumbs into the palm of the glove, up towards the wrist portion.

2. Next, have students stuff as many plastic bags or newspaper into the remaining fingers as possible, so they become the arms and the legs of their puppet. Have them stuff the palm as well, stopping at the wrist.

3. Using the wire, tie the top at the base of the wrist, closest to the palm, to form the head. The thumb of the glove should already be stuffed inside, giving it enough padding (no need to stuff plastic bags or newspaper for the head).

4. Have students use the fabric and other collage elements to dress and decorate their puppet. They can make clothing, hats, hair, props, etc. to dress their puppet.

GLOSSARY

1. Aboriginal – (Of human races, animals, and plants) inhabiting or existing in a land from the earliest times or from before the arrival of colonists; indigenous. Relating to the Australian Aborigines or their languages.

2. Alien - Supposedly from another world; extraterrestrial.

3. Bridge (as it pertains to the nose) - The upper bony part of a person's nose.

4. Composition - The artistic arrangement of the parts of a picture.

5. Complimentary Color - one of a pair of primary or secondary colors opposed to the other member of the pair on a schematic chart or scale.

6. Contour - An outline representing or bounding the shape or form of something.

7. Crease - A line or ridge produced on paper or cloth by folding, pressing, or crushing.

8. Divide - Separate or be separated into parts.

9. Diorama - A model representing a scene with three-dimensional figures, either in miniature or as a large-scale museum exhibit.

10. Horizontal - Parallel to the plane of the horizon; at right angles to the vertical.

11. Impression - a mark or design on (an object) using a stamp or seal.

12. Layers - A sheet, quantity, or thickness of material, typically one of several, covering a surface or body.

13. Muslin - Lightweight cotton cloth in a plain weave.

14. Oil Pastels – a painting and drawing medium in stick form, from a mixture of pigments, non-drying oil, and wax binder; also called oil crayon.

15. Overlap – Extend over so as to cover partly.

16. Pattern – A repeated decorate design.

17. Pop-art - Art based on modern popular culture and the mass media, especially as a critical or ironic comment on traditional fine art values.

18. Puppet - A movable model of a person or animal that is typically moved either by strings controlled from above or by a hand inside it.

19. Reconstruct - Build or form (something) again after it has been damaged or destroyed

20. Relief - A method of moulding, carving, or stamping in which the design stands out from the surface, to a greater (high relief) or lesser (low relief) extent.

21. Repeat – Say or do the same thing again.

22. Represent - Depict (a particular subject) in a work of art.

23. Segment - Each of the parts into which something is or may be divided.

24. Surrealism - A 20th-century avant-garde movement in art and literature which sought to release the creative potential of the unconscious mind, for example by the irrational juxtaposition of images.

25. Textile - A type of cloth or woven fabric.

26. Three-dimensional - Having or appearing to have length, breadth, and depth.

27. Transfer - Move from one place to another.

28. Zentangle – an easy-to-learn art form using a method of creating images from structured patterns. Developed by Maria Thomas and Rock Roberts of Zentangle Inc.

SOURCES

1. "Aboriginal - Definition of Aboriginal in English | Oxford Dictionaries." N.p., n.d. Web. 26 Apr. 2017.

2. "Aboriginal Mask | Crayola.com." N.p., n.d. Web. 26 Apr. 2017.

3. "Alien - Definition of Alien in English | Oxford Dictionaries." N.p., n.d. Web. 26 Apr. 2017.

4. Biography.com Editors. "Salvador Dalí Biography.com." A&E Television Networks. N.p., 2016. Web. 26 Apr. 2017.

5. "Bridge - Definition of Bridge in English | Oxford Dictionaries." N.p., n.d. Web. 26 Apr. 2017.

6. "Cesar Domela, Notes of Biography." N.p., n.d. Web. 26 Apr. 2017.

7. "Charles Fazzino's Biography." N.p., n.d. Web. 26 Apr. 2017.

8. "Complementary Color | Define Complementary Color at Dictionary.com." N.p., n.d. Web. 26 Apr. 2017.

9. "Composition - Definition of Composition in English | Oxford Dictionaries." N.p., n.d. Web. 26 Apr. 2017.

10. "Contour - Definition of Contour in English | Oxford Dictionaries." N.p., n.d. Web. 26 Apr. 2017.

11. "Crease - Definition of Crease in English | Oxford Dictionaries." N.p., n.d. Web. 26 Apr. 2017.

12. "Diorama - Definition of Diorama in English | Oxford Dictionaries." N.p., n.d. Web. 26 Apr. 2017.

13. "Divide - Definition of Divide in English | Oxford Dictionaries." N.p., n.d. Web. 26 Apr. 2017.

14. "Ed Emberley - Wikipedia." N.p., 2017. Web. 26 Apr. 2017.

15. "Famous 3D Pop Art Artist; Charles Fazzino | Fazzino." N.p., n.d. Web. 26 Apr. 2017.

16. "Horizontal - Definition of Horizontal in English | Oxford Dictionaries." N.p., n.d. Web. 26 Apr. 2017.

17. "Impress - Definition of Impress in English | Oxford Dictionaries." N.p., n.d. Web. 26 Apr. 2017.

18. "Layer - Definition of Layer in English | Oxford Dictionaries." N.p., n.d. Web. 26 Apr. 2017.

19. "Muslin - Definition of Muslin in English | Oxford Dictionaries." N.p., n.d. Web. 26 Apr. 2017.

20. "Oil Pastel | Define Oil Pastel at Dictionary.com." N.p., n.d. Web. 26 Apr. 2017.

21. "Overlap - Definition of Overlap in English | Oxford Dictionaries." N.p., n.d. Web. 26 Apr. 2017.

22. "Pattern - Definition of Pattern in English | Oxford Dictionaries." N.p., n.d. Web. 26 Apr. 2017.

23. "Pop Art - Definition of Pop Art in English | Oxford Dictionaries." N.p., n.d. Web. 26 Apr. 2017.

24. "Puppet - Definition of Puppet in English | Oxford Dictionaries." N.p., n.d. Web. 26 Apr. 2017.

25. "Reconstruct - Definition of Reconstruct in English | Oxford Dictionaries." N.p., n.d. Web. 26 Apr. 2017.

26. "Relief - Definition of Relief in English | Oxford Dictionaries." N.p., n.d. Web. 26 Apr. 2017.

27. "Repeat - Definition of Repeat in English | Oxford Dictionaries." N.p., n.d. Web. 26 Apr. 2017.

28. "Represent - Definition of Represent in English | Oxford Dictionaries." N.p., n.d. Web. 26 Apr. 2017.

Resture, Jane. "Australia - Aboriginal Art, Culture And Landscape." N.p., n.d. Web. 26 Apr. 2017.

29. "ROMERO BRITTO - Biography." N.p., n.d. Web. 26 Apr. 2017.

30. "Segment - Definition of Segment in English | Oxford Dictionaries." N.p., n.d. Web. 26 Apr. 2017.

31. "Surrealism - Definition of Surrealism in English | Oxford Dictionaries." N.p., n.d. Web. 26 Apr. 2017.

32. "Textile - Definition of Textile in English | Oxford Dictionaries." N.p., n.d. Web. 26 Apr. 2017.

33. "The Arts of Life - Zentangle." The Arts of Life. N.p., 2011. Web. 26 Apr. 2017.

34. "Three-Dimensional - Definition of Three-Dimensional in English | Oxford Dictionaries." N.p., n.d. Web. 26 Apr. 2017.

35. "Transfer - Definition of Transfer in English | Oxford Dictionaries." N.p., n.d. Web. 26 Apr. 2017.

36. Violatti, Cristian. "Mandala - Ancient History Encyclopedia." N.p., 2017. Web. 26 Apr. 2017.

ACKNOWLEDGMENTS

Many thanks to Ron Kohler for proofreading the book.

Thank you Bess Gutter for continuing to work on this project.

Thank you to all the teachers and students who participated in Creative Adventures programs and always inspiring me!

Thank you to my mother, Denise, for instilling me with a love of all things education.

To my father, Sam, and his inspiring pep talks and dad jokes.

To my sister, Rachel, for being the toughest woman I know.

And to my dog, Luna, for keeping me company while I worked (and she slept).